A Police Officer's Guide and Handbook to Tactical Casualty Care (Under Fire)

RAFAEL NAVARRO

Copyright © 2010 Rafael Navarro

All rights reserved.

ISBN:1-4637-0951-X
ISBN-13: 978-1-4637-0951-8

DEDICATION

In honor of the men and women (brothers and sisters) in law enforcement all over this county, and to those of us who during the performance of the ever so dedicated profession we share, were made to make the ultimate sacrifice. There is something to learn from what has been communicated to us. Let not a single one of those tragic lessons be unheard or unlearned. To the vast cadre of police instructors, law enforcement medics, and associations who have dedicated their cause in the support of law enforcement survival. To my wife Kami and our children; for their patience and support during my twenty one years of military service and the past ten years as a law enforcement officer.

CONTENTS

	Acknowledgements..	I
	Preface..	II
	Forward..	III
1	Concepts, Goals and Relevance of Tactical Casualty Care to The Law Enforcement Community...	p3
2	Three Stages of Care During a Critical Incident and Factors that Influence This Care..	p12
3	Distinguishing the Difference Between Life Threatening and Non-Life Threatening Injuries...	p15
4	Understanding When and Where to Treat Life Threatening and Non-Life Threatening Injuries...	p18
5	The Application and Use of Field Dressings, Pressure Dressings, and Tourniquets..	p23
6	Recommendations for Assembling a "Gunshot Kit".........................	p29
7	Techniques for Moving Casualties...	p32
8	Scenario Based, Realistic and Dynamic Training...............................	p39
9	Sample Lesson Plan..	p44
10	Sample Scenario Script with Timeline...	p49

ACKNOWLEDGMENTS

I would like to thank Sam L. Slick, PhD, for his genuine mentoring and belief in this project as well as Matt, Sztajnkrycer, MD, PhD, for his dedicated research and the creation and management of his web site (valorproject.org). Special thanks to my colleague Bill Byrd, who has in many ways supported my ideas and with his tremendous efforts in the development and implementation of this book. Finally, the eternal gratefulness I owe to Kami Navarro, my wife, for her encouragement and support throughout all of my military deployments and my current quest to communicate, educate and save lives.

Preface

To the officer ... It is my goal to provide you with information that may save your life or the life of the person next to you. I have endeavored to package and present this material in the most basic fashion. I am determined to share the concepts, knowledge, and techniques currently being applied in both the military and some law enforcement agencies; of course without the complicated terminology. It is intended to be easily read, learned, retained, and reviewed. Therefore, in most cases you will notice I am relating the information for you, through the "lingo" and the "eyes" of a police officer.

To the police trainer ... We share the same passion. As you are aware, the profession you and I share mixes the responsibilities, legal requirements, and mandatory certifications of law enforcement with the responsibilities, organization requirements, and goal orientation of an educator. In my opinion, there is no better occupational satisfaction other than witnessing the results of your hard work and the work of your colleagues as one of your own, surviving a violent encounter or simply preventing one from occurring through the use of good judgment.

Disclaimer - Use this book to learn from, teach from, as a source for "hip pocket training", as a gateway to more educational resources, and as context for future practice advances which will better prepare you for the challenges we face. Keep in mind, the intent of this book is for educational purposes only. All medical tactics, techniques, and procedures should be discussed with, and approved by your department medical director.

The guidelines, recommendations, and procedures provided are based on the fast-paced, ever-changing practice of medicine. Information provided at the time of publication is the latest available. By the time of publishing, some of this information may very well be out-of-date; therefore I cannot accept responsibility for discrepancies.

**If no one has reminded you lately:
You are the tip of the spear! Stay safe, stay sharp and stay around to enjoy your life!**

**Deputy Trainer Shawn Pappas
Pinellas County Sheriff's Office**

Forward

Rafael and I have both worn military, law enforcement, and SWAT uniforms. We served together for many years on the same entry team and have taught together in the classroom. Rafael has dedicated his life to serving others; first to his wife and children but also to the calling of protecting his country and community.

His desire to serve and protect has now come full circle while taking on the task of teaching fellow law enforcement officers how to protect themselves. When I learned of his endeavor to teach combat casualty care, my first thought was 'why haven't we been doing this already'.

I was recently seriously injured while on duty but fortunately, paramedics were on scene when it happened. In fact, I literally landed on one of them when I hit the ground! Because of this, my treatment was swift, receiving morphine and being swept away in an ambulance in less than five minutes. Most cases don't happen like this so it is imperative that we know how to self-treat these serious events or provide care to our brothers and sisters, ensuring we live to fight another day.

This book is an integral part of your officer safety plan. Having a plan and the knowledge of what to do when that critical event occurs will mean the difference between a hero's welcome home or putting another name on a memorial. We can no longer say "I don't know what I'll do, but I'm sure I'll do the right thing". It is our responsibility to know what we will do when our moment arrives.

I hope you appreciate the work Rafael has invested in this venture by reading, understanding, and continuing your training. Treat every day like it is a gift and take responsibility for yourself and the officers you stand with. We need you out there, your family trusts you'll be home tonight, and the fight is not over.

Bill Byrd

Chapter 1

Concepts, Goals and Relevance of Tactical Casualty Care to The Law Enforcement Community

As police officers, every single day we are faced with the reality of violent encounters on our streets and within our communities. At times, they become high profile encounters.

November 29, 2009

Four members of the Lakewood, WA Police Department were shot and killed in an ambush attack as they sat in a coffee shop catching up on paperwork and planning for their upcoming shift. A lone gunman walked in and opened fire on the officers, who were in full uniform and wearing protective body armor.

March 21, 2009

Four members of the Oakland, CA Police Department were shot and killed by the same gunman in two related incidents. Sergeant Mark Dunakin and Officer John Hege, both motorcycle officers, were shot following a traffic stop in East Oakland. Just over two hours later, SWAT team members, responding to an anonymous tip, tracked the gunman to an apartment building just a few blocks from the original shooting scene. As they entered a bedroom, the gunman opened fire through a closet with an assault weapon.

September 11, 2001

On this, the deadliest day in U.S. law enforcement history, 72 officers were killed as a result of the terrorist attacks on America. 71 of the officers died while responding to the attacks on the World Trade Center in lower Manhattan, including 37 members of the Port Authority Police Departments from New York and New Jersey. That represented the single largest loss of law enforcement personnel by a single agency in U.S. history. Also killed at the World Trade Center were 23 members of the New York City Police Department, 5 members of the New York State Department of Taxation and Finance, 3 members of the New York State Office of Court Administration, and 1 law enforcement member each from the New York City Fire Department, Federal Bureau of Investigation, and U.S. Secret Service. In addition, a U.S. Fish and Wildlife Service officer died in the crash of United Flight 93 outside Shanksville, PA.

Many times, these violent encounters never make it to a high profile national media status, but they do directly affect you.

October 9th 2001

2210hrs; Corporal Terry Metts is dispatched to a "shots fired" call in the Lealman area of Pinellas County, FL. During the initial stages of this call, Cpl. Metts is shot with a high powered rifle. Cpl. Metts advises that he is shot in his arm and bleeding profusely. The efforts to rescue Cpl. Metts were initially hampered due to responding deputies being pinned down by gun fire. Cpl. Metts was able to apply direct pressure to his wounds, and despite severe blood loss, was able to shoot out a street light, which aided his rescuers and ultimately survive this incident. Cpl. Metts quickly recognized the onset of shock and was able to combat this as well, and maintain his composure in a terrifying situation.

January 24, 2011

St. Petersburg, FL, two police officers died and a federal marshal was injured in a shootout with a violent fugitive sex offender. The department identified the slain officers as Tom Baitinger, 48, a 14-year department veteran, and Jeffrey Yaslowitz, 39, an 11-year veteran.

By the time this book goes through its final phase and distribution, some of the information provided will be outdated, meaning unfortunately, the numbers will probably be higher.

The reporting numbers that follow have been taken from the U.S. Department of Justice, Federal Bureau of Investigation released October 2010.

From the October 2010 report, the following were from the category of 'law enforcement officers feloniously killed'.

- In 2009, 48 law enforcement officers were feloniously killed in the line of duty.

- Thirty-two of the slain officers were employed by city police departments. Of these, nearly half (15) were with law enforcement agencies in cities with 250,000 or more inhabitants.

- Line-of-duty deaths occurred in 18 states and Puerto Rico.

- Twenty-one officers lost their lives in the South. Thirteen officers died in the West, 7 died in the Northeast, and 5 officers who were feloniously slain, were employed in the Midwest.

- The average age of officers who were feloniously killed in 2009 was 38 years.

The slain officers' average length of law enforcement service was 12 years.

Of the 48 officers slain in 2009, 47 were male and 1 was female. Forty-two of the victim officers were white, 3 were black, 2 were American Indian/Alaskan Native and 1 officer was Asian/Pacific Islander.

- 15 officers died in ambush situations.

- 8 officers died from felonious attacks during arrest situations.

- 8 officers died during traffic pursuits/stops.

- 6 officers died answering disturbance calls.

- 5 officers died during tactical situations (barricaded offender, hostage taking, etc.).

- 4 officers died while investigating suspicious persons/circumstances.

- 2 officers were killed while transporting or maintaining custody of prisoners.

-
- 35 officers who were slain in 2009 were assigned to vehicle patrol.

- 2 of the slain officers were off duty but were acting in an official capacity.

- 11 officers were assigned to other duties, such as special assignments or undercover, when they were murdered.

Weapons

Most officers slain in 2009 (45 of the 48) were killed with firearms. Of those killed with firearms, 28 were killed with handguns.

- 2 officers were killed with their own weapons.

- 9 officers attempted to use their weapons. 12 officers were able to fire their weapons.

- 19 officers were slain with firearms when they were 0-5 feet from the offenders.

Body Armor

Most of the officers feloniously killed in 2009 (36 of the 48 officers) were wearing body armor at the time of their murder. Of the 36, 33 officers who were wearing body armor were killed with firearms.

- 12 suffered wounds to the front of the head.

- 7 were wounded in the front upper torso.

- 6 were shot in the neck/throat.

- 5 were shot in the side of the head.

- 2 were shot in the back of the head.

- 1 officer was shot in the back.

Months, days, and times of incidents

More officers (8) died from felonious assaults that occurred in April than in any other month. 13 officers were involved in fatal assaults which occurred on Saturday; more than on any other day of the week.

More officers (13) were fatally injured in assaults that happened from 8:01 p.m. to midnight than during any other time period.

Offenders

In 2009, 41 alleged offenders were identified in connection with the 48 law enforcement officers feloniously killed. Of those offenders, the following characteristics are known:

- The average age of the alleged offenders was 32 years old.

- The average height was 5 feet 10 inches tall, and the average weight was 181 pounds.

- 39 of the alleged offenders were male; 2 were female.

- 24 of the alleged offenders were white and 17 were black.

- 33 of the 41 offenders had prior criminal arrests.

- 13 of the alleged offenders were under judicial supervision at the time of the incidents.

- 2 of the alleged offenders were intoxicated or under the influence of alcohol at the time of the fatal incidents.

I am almost certain we would all agree, the general perception within the law enforcement community is that lately, things are just getting really dangerous for cops. Take another look at those statistics. How many of these officers did we really need to lose? Every one of those numbers represents someone like you and me.

When you read and learn about each of these violent encounters specifically, whether it's an armed encounter (ambush) or a physical hand to hand encounter, you might learn that unfortunately, there are in fact those that even a "well-trained officer" would not have survived.

However, (with sincere respect to our fallen) as you further study these encounters, you will also discover a number of these could have been survivable, if there had been some additional training and or equipment.

When I mention additional training, I'm not referring to your scheduled in-service training.

I am specifically referring to scenario based, attitude changing, muscle memory training, which creates a reasonable amount of stress, mimicking your body's reaction during a violent encounter.

Any law enforcement instructor "RED SHIRT" specialized in high liability subjects will tell you, the only way to be ready for a violent encounter is to maintain a series of skill sets, which result in a desired response during a stressful or life-threatening event.

Most of us have heard of this as creating muscle memory under stress. As a result, the physiological aspects created from this type of training shape our thinking and perception of the world we live and work in. We experience and defend against violence and therefore this prepares us to always be cautious. These same instructors will also tell you, the ultimate challenge to the officer is not the "bad guy", but the officer themselves. In other words, complacency!

Several well written books have covered this subject very thoroughly but I have yet to find one that covers the subject of care under fire dedicated for the officer on patrol or who is not part of a specialized team.

So, what about the officer who does not have access to these skills through their department? Look to encourage your department to consider more training to support such an event. Have updated information on the reasons it would be beneficial for both the officers and the department. Have a basic understanding of the concepts, goals and how all of these relate to the agency before you suggest the training.

Concepts and definitions

Tactical casualty care is the pre-hospital care given by you for yourself, or to another officer in a tactical, ambush, or otherwise combat-like environment. These principles are different from those of traditional "civilian trauma care" because they are based on both the unique types of wounds which are suffered here and the tactical conditions faced.

The unique wounds (gunshot) and tactical conditions (actions carefully planned to gain a specific end) make it difficult to determine which intervention to perform at what time.

Tactical care under fire is the care rendered by the rescuer at the point of injury while he and the casualty are still under fire.

The risk of additional injuries at any moment is extremely high for both the casualty and the rescuer. Performing a life-saving technique at the wrong time or place, may be worse for both the victim and the rescuer.

The major considerations during this phase are as follows:

- Suppression of the suspect's fire.

- Moving yourself or the casualty to a safe position.

- Treatment of immediate life-threatening bleeding.

Tactical casualty care goals

These goals represent a system to manage your injuries or the injuries of another, taking in consideration the concepts previously discussed. An important guiding principle is the performance of the correct procedure at the right time.

In order to keep this simple, here are three goals:

- Treat yourself or the casualty (self-treatment or buddy aid).

- Prevent additional injuries or casualties.

- Complete the mission (officer rescue).

Treating yourself or the casualty is dependent strictly your skills and the equipment you currently have access to. Taking a traditional approach (your ABC's) may not be the most appropriate course of action. However, being able to quickly identify a life-threatening injury can make the difference.

The prevention of additional injuries is dependent on the rate of the suspect's fire, your ability to defend or return fire, current equipment, surroundings, your mobility, and the decision of when and where to address the injuries.

The completion of the mission may not involve the initial call itself. In the military for example, a mission may be to take a hill at all costs. Whereas in the law enforcement arena, if I am dispatched to a noise complaint but I am ambushed and have sustained injuries, my mission is to stay alive, and that will, now become my only mission. Live to fight another day!

The "Warrior Mindset", or a mindset that one will not ever give up or ever die, is paramount during this event. It may be the difference between death (giving up) and survival (never giving up). Do you have the willingness to injure, or kill if necessary, to preserve your life?

According to author Jerry Van Cook, (Real World Self-Defense, Paladin Press, 1999) successfully defending yourself is the result of approximately 99% psychological and 1% training. Focus on your primary objective of survival. The warrior mindset is more important than any polished technique.

When faced with attack, act immediately and escape. Do not let anything get in your way of survival. Never, ever give up! The essential components of the warrior mindset are:

- Toughness
- Immediate Response
- Focus

Toughness

Mental and physical toughness means being absolutely ruthless in your defense. You act without compassion, pity, or mercy against an attacker who wants to violate you. You become an animal, propelled by indignant rage.

Immediate Response

Respond immediately with the appropriate level of force. Stop the attack and escape. A warrior does not wait as the advantage is in the surprise of instant and direct offense. Most criminals expect their victims to be in fear and comply. Do the opposite and resist quickly and forcefully.

Focus

Stay focused and single-minded on your goal of survival. Be persistent and continue to respond if first response is not effective. Commit to your goal of survival and let nothing get in your way.

The warrior mindset, or mental development, must progress with physical training. Without some balance, you either are overly confident and cannot execute a physical response, or are extremely skilled but mentally unable to exercise your techniques.

First Aid - The immediate Aid given to a casualty prior to the arrival of medical personnel (EMS).

Non-life threatening injuries- Injuries that will not require any immediate action by the injured or another to sustain life (NOT SICK).

Life threatening injuries- injuries which will require an immediate action by an injured person or another, in order to prevent death (SICK).

Chapter 2

Three Stages of Care During a Critical Incident and Factors that Influence This Care

'Care during a critical incident' is a broad brush statement so to make this simple, I have broken it down into three stages:

Tactical Care Under Fire
Tactical Field Care
Medical or Casualty Evacuation Care

Tactical care under fire, as discussed previously, is best described as what you and I can do for ourselves, right now, before we die. Access to medical personal and equipment is not available. The potential of further injury or death is high if we don't identify and make quick life-saving decisions.

During this stage, it is best to follow a simple plan. This plan needs to be rehearsed, both in your mind and during scenario based training. It needs to be fluid and based on the factors surrounding the encounter. These factors can be, but are not limited to the suspect(s) intent, position, mobility, and weaponry.

Basic Management Plan for Care Under Fire

- Return fire and take cover immediately. Remember unlike the "bad guys" we are responsible for each of our rounds.
- Direct or expect your fellow officer to remain engaged by defending or taking action against the suspect if appropriate.
- Try to keep yourself, or your fellow officer, from sustaining additional wounds.
- Airway management is addressed during the tactical field care phase.
- Stop life-threatening external hemorrhaging if tactically feasible by directing your fellow officer to control the hemorrhage by self-aid if able.
- Use a tourniquet for a hemorrhage that is appropriate to tourniquet application.
- Apply the tourniquet proximal to the bleeding site, over the uniform, tighten, and move yourself or the officer to cover.

This basic management plan is considered, in my opinion, to be the base line. If there is nothing more retained in your memory from this book, have this plan in your memory's rolodex. No matter how much training or highly technical skills you possess, it may not make a difference if quick action is not taken. This book will focus on how to become proficient during in this phase.

Tactical field care is the care rendered by an officer or medic once he or she is no longer in the line of fire. This also applies to situations in which an injury has occurred, but there has been no hostile fire. Available medical equipment is still limited to that carried into the field by the deputies or medical personnel assigned to the team.

During this stage, airway management can be addressed. Further assessments can be provided by trained personnel like police medics and/or tactical emergency medical services (TEMS). They are, for the most part, tactical paramedics trained to save lives in high-risk situations and provide patient care, first aid and administer drugs to those who are seriously injured. The field of tactical medicine is designed for those who are working with law enforcement officers, departments and agencies in situations where there is a high risk of life-threatening injuries.

Most SWAT teams or teams of this nature, have TEMS personnel in place and spend hours upon hours, practicing their chosen discipline.

Casualty evacuation care, also known as CASEVAC, is a military acronym for the emergency patient evacuation of casualties from a combat zone. CASEVAC can be done by either ground or air. CASEVAC vehicles are non-standardized and non-dedicated vehicles, which do not necessarily have en route care capabilities. This would translate in the law enforcement community as any vehicle, other than an ambulance or medical helicopter. The primary difference between a CASEVAC and a medical evacuation (MEDEVAC) is a MEDEVAC uses a standardized and dedicated vehicle, providing en route care.

If we think back to the North Hollywood Shootings, we recall seeing city vehicles, dump trucks and even private armored vehicles being used to rescue and move the injured from the line of fire. The lessons learned there have led agencies throughout the world to develop SOP's on officer rescues.

Many agencies require medical transport to be summoned to your location to transport an injured person. Some agencies don't address the issue at all. Think about this for a moment; would a violation of your agency's policy be justified to save the life of a fellow officer?

In other words, are you allowed to transport casualties in your police vehicle? Have you considered how you would do this if required? Do you know what your agency policy says about this? I am not recommending you violate your agency policies, just like no "RED SHIRT" will ever tell you when you can shoot your weapon or use deadly force.

Your articulation of the facts known to you at the time and the circumstances surrounding the event will need to justify your actions.

Remember the Warrior Mindset!

Chapter 3

Distinguishing the Difference Between Life Threatening and Non-Life Threatening Injuries

As I have mentioned several times before, making a quick assessment of the injuries will play a major role in our survival.

As a police officer, you are not expected to have a medical background, nor am I suggesting officers should have one. Most police officers, however; are required to hold basic certifications in subjects like CPR and First Aid. This can definitely be an advantage.

It must be clear that the conditions which are presented while under fire change the priorities that are commonly listed in a first aid course. The urgency for quick movement, addressing the threat and communication of our assessment may not allow the luxury of following all the "course recommended" steps.

Your assessment should involve a "triage" like approach. Under these conditions (care under fire) it comes down to SICK or NOT SICK.

Sick is a term that is widely used in our country. In this context, however; an officer described as SICK, implies the officer is critically injured and will die in the next 15-20 minutes. In other words, he has sustained life threatening injuries. These injuries will require immediate action by the injured officer or another, in order to prevent death.

Not sick is also a commonly used term. In the care under fire context, an officer described as NOT SICK, implies that while injured, the officer will survive for at least the immediate time being. Therefore, the officer has sustained non-life threatening injuries. These injuries will not require any immediate action by the injured or another, to sustain life.

I often ask students if they should obtain this status from the injured officer, either by radio or by calling out to them. Most reply, it would appear to be the most appropriate.

I then ask them to consider the officer who has that "Warrior Mindset" and if that officer will likely admit, or allow themselves to believe, he or she is SICK? I certainly do not want them to.

In other words, we have to be very careful while obtaining this information. If while providing psychological first aid over the radio, telling the officer that you are on the way, you can determine their status, then good. I recommend you don't ask the officer their triage status, because in their mind, they should be saying they will survive!

Keep in mind, the officer's status is just one factor in your hasty rescue plan. Do not allow yourself to become emotionally involved and get drawn into becoming another victim. If this occurs, you won't be able to perform the rescue, and now a second rescue (for you) will be required. Think scene safety!

Basic facts to help determining if your officer is SICK or NOT SICK

The average adult male has 4-5 quarts of blood in their body. Blood pressure begins to drop (hypotension) when about 30% of that blood is lost. Death can occur when >40% of blood loss occurs and the volume is not replaced.

Large amounts of blood loss can cause shock. Because the average police officer is not a medic, carrying medical supplies and equipment, the areas where we can control large amounts of bleeding, while under fire, are limited.

In preparing yourself to identify and treat different types of bleeding, you must first have a good understanding of the three distinct types of bleeding a person can experience.

Capillary Bleeding - when a minor scrape or cut opens capillaries. Capillary bleeding is almost always very slow and small in quantity. Your body's natural clotting mechanism is able to stop most cases of capillary bleeding within seconds to minutes.

Venous Bleeding - deep cuts have the potential to cut open veins. A cut vein typically results in a steady but relatively slow flow of dark red blood. The best way to stop most cases of venous bleeding is to put direct pressure on the wound.

Arterial Bleeding - is the least common and most dangerous type of bleeding. This involves bright red blood that comes out in large volumes, and in spurts that correspond with each beat of the heart.

In cases of arterial bleeding, direct and extremely firm pressure on the wound is the best way of stopping it. If direct pressure is not applied, a severe arterial wound can cause one to bleed to death within a few minutes.

Extremity injuries can vary from a complete amputation to small punctures wounds. The key here is to focus on the type of bleeding. Considerations as to how to, or what to use to control the bleeding, depends on the type of bleeding and the threat(s) presented.

People, who are fatally shot, typically die from injuries like severe blood loss caused from a severed artery or damage to a vital organ. Shooting victims also succumb to tension pneumothorax (collapsed lung), spinal cord injuries, or severe brain damage. You can't be expected to know which one the person is suffering from. All you need to do is look for the obvious life threatening injuries, and treat these appropriately.

In the following chapter, we will focus primarily on the extremity, abdominal and chest injuries. Please keep in mind, the setting of our violent encounter limits us to what we can do, however; with the "Warrior Mindset", some inexpensive equipment and a little know how, we can increase our survival rates significantly.

CHAPTER 4

Understanding When and Where to Treat Life Threatening and Non-Life Threatening Injuries

While responding to a call, I am approaching the home when I am encountered by gunfire. I am injured, sustaining a venous bleed (very minor/slow flow). I should:

- Return fire and take cover immediately (no specific order)
- Remain engaged, by defending or taking action against the suspect if appropriate (avoid additional wounds)
- Control hemorrhage by self-aid if able
- If the threat is still present and engaging, one handed direct pressure or the quick application of a tourniquet can be used to control the blood loss
- Continually assess, move if needed and communicate to dispatch

During the care under fire phase, the casualty and rescuer remain in grave danger from hostile fire. While your assessment can be immediately obtained, your application of a life-saving technique(s) may have to wait until you are out of the line of fire.

3 RISK PHASES

If you're making an approach to the same house with another officer, a very different situation exists than what a rescuer might think of. If you're right next to an officer who goes down, it's much easier to grab him and move him to safety ASAP, rather than retreat without him only to try to rescue him later.

If, however; a rescue can't be effected instantly for some reason, or if you and others arrive after an officer is already down, you are then challenged by the 3 phases of risk, so long as there's still a potential active threat.

- The Approach - Risk Phase exists for the time and distance required for you to penetrate into the "kill zone" from your last point of cover and concealment to the downed officer.

- The Aid - Risk Phase consists of the time you spend in the "kill zone", under threat of effective fire, assessing the downed officer and performing preliminary care.

- This phase is high risk because a suspect will likely be aware of the rescue attempt, the team is relatively static, and situational awareness is easily lost while focusing on the injured officer.

- The Extraction - Risk Phase covers the time and distance necessary for you to move from the "kill zone" and to a position of relative safety, where further medical aid and definitive evacuation can be performed."

I previously mentioned, it is important to keep in mind that the officers' status is only one factor in your hasty rescue plan. Do not allow yourself to become emotionally involved and get drawn into becoming another victim, which would result in the need to plan and perform a second rescue.

Instead, wait for a few moments and assess the risks vs. benefits of each of these phases. Think about potential safe areas before launching into action.

You're probably thinking, "easier said than done" And I would agree. The chances, however; are pretty good that if you know an officer is down, then the suspect probably also knows this as well. The suspect may have a plan for what he'll do when a rescue is attempted. Keep in mind; you may have to take care of the threat first! In many situations, this would in fact be considered the most appropriate care.

APPROACH CONSIDERATIONS

An important consideration to remember would be to attempt to discover, as quickly as you can, if your are actually dealing with a downed-officer rescue or a body recovery. If this can be determined prior to the deployment of your rescue element, you may very well avoid unnecessary casualties.

Since hands-on assessment isn't possible, look for indirect signs of life, such as spontaneous movement, spontaneous chest rise, or exhaled breath on a cold day. Exposed brain matter from head wounds strongly suggests a fatality, although such wounds have proven survivable in many cases. If available on scene, the use of observation equipment, such as binoculars to assess the victim, can provide real time intelligence.

If the downed officer is judged to be dead, then a decision to slow everything down should be considered. When the situation has been resolved, a safe recovery of the officer can be performed.

As mentioned before, with an officer who appears to be alive, you need to determine if he is "SICK" or "NOT SICK". This decision is important as we noted that a SICK patient requires immediate action.

If the officer is awake and able to move, order the officer to initiate self-aid as appropriate, while awaiting rescue. Unfortunately, many people equate being shot with being helpless or dead, something frequently reinforced in training. Nothing could be further from the truth.

Once injured, some officers may simply shut down. Forcefully remind them that they need to fight and that they are not allowed to give up. If the injury requires simple emergency treatment, such as applying pressure to a wound to decrease bleeding, tell them to do that. Depending on their injury, they may be able to provide cover for the rescue team. They certainly should be asked to provide intelligence on the situation, thereby keeping them engaged and actively involved in their own survival.

AID CONSIDERATIONS

In a high-threat situation, medical care should be extremely limited. It is best advised to focus only on extrication, and as a result, minimizing exposure and risk. The only medical care given while in the line of fire should be to control life-threatening hemorrhage, achieved through the rapid use of a tourniquet. As a general rule, tourniquet placement should take no more than 7-10 seconds.

Several different types of tourniquets are available on the market today. Your selection of a tourniquet should at least involve a little research. Consider which ones are proven pieces of equipment. Also consider their size and where they can be carried. Most extremity bleeding can be controlled with direct pressure. When bleeding is uncontrolled with pressure, a tourniquet should be used.

Abdominal bleeding is more concerning. Heavy bleeding can occur with very little visual confirmation. For the most part, the sooner you can get the officer to emergency care, the better. These injuries are difficult to treat in the care under fire phase. Attempt to apply direct pressure to these wounds as you rapidly move the casualty to cover. Once under cover, a hemostatic agent such as "Quik Clot" is appropriate for these injuries.

Heavy chest bleeding can come from the blood vessels which run from the center of the chest cavity up to the head and down to the abdomen. The heart and lungs can also be involved which will bleed heavily.

The rib cage can also bleed if one of the blood vessels underneath each rib is injured but this bleeding tends to be at a slower rate.

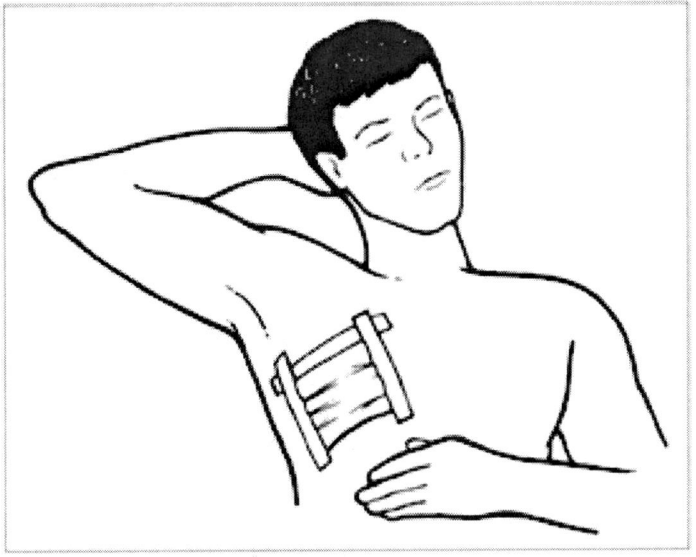

A partially, airtight seal should be applied to chest injuries as soon as possible to help prevent a collapsed lung. Vaseline gauze or the inside of your bandage wrapper can be used but any clean, airtight material may be used. Your rain coat or hat liner can be quickly cut to fit this situation. Apply the airtight bandage on three sides of the wound (see image above). Do not close the bandage on the fourth side. This will create a natural valve which will allow the chest to achieve its usual negative pressure state. Air will escape through the valve during inhalation. Like the abdominal injury, quick transport to surgery is the best option.

EXTRACTION CONSIDERATIONS

Removing a downed officer can take twice as long as the approach. This is, in part, due to a victim who cannot help themselves and unable to assist in movement.

To minimize risk, an appropriate extraction route, with suitable points of cover, should be determined before initiating the rescue. During this phase, if you cannot remove the officer to a point of definitive safety, it may be safer to move him to a position of relative safety. Here, additional care can be rendered, while the elimination of the threat can be accomplished.

An example of this could be simply moving your officer around a building, behind a vehicle or out of the suspect's field of fire.

Scenarios like this were once thought to be unlikely. Unfortunately, we have seen that this is certainly not the case anymore. Therefore, it is strongly recommended you carry (as a minimum) some type of approved tourniquet on your person. Your tourniquet should also be accessible with either hand and from a variety of positions.

Additional thoughts

- Sick or Not Sick? (who made the assessment?)
- Where is my downed officer? (injured officers can be confused)
- Are you running into an ambush?
- Do you know what your ballistic shield is rated for?
- Do you know what your ballistic vest is rated for?
- Will carrying a ballistic shield to the rescue hamper your movement? (movement vs. cover)

While there are many more areas to consider, these are a few I have seen to have been major factors needing consideration when putting your hasty rescue plan together.

Avoid errors like assignment of duties and responsibilities within a quickly assembled team of officers. This can lead to confusion and further casualties. Encourage your agency to set training time for officer rescue training. It is difficult to expect a person to perform correctly under stress unless some training has been experienced.

If your suspect is mobile, you should worry about the angles. Your approach and return from the kill zone, should be very fluid as well.

Understand your return from the rescue may take twice as long as the approach. This is because you will be carrying a brother, fighting fatigue and trying to maintain your team integrity.

CHAPTER 5

The Application and Use of Field Dressings, Pressure Dressings, and Tourniquets

If an officer is losing blood from a wound, you must take measures to control the bleeding. A field dressing can be applied to any wound which is bleeding heavily. If the wound is on an arm or leg, a pressure dressing can also be applied. If the bleeding still doesn't stop, a tourniquet can be placed around an upper arm or thigh, and then tightened to stop the flow of blood below the band.

As we discussed in a Chapter Four, Care Under Fire, the decision of where and what to use are dependent on the situation.

If your agency provides field dressings or your officers are self-purchasing them, we still have to consider if they will have access to them when they need them. Unlike the recommendation given for the tourniquet, both field dressings and pressure dressings are usually kept in some kind of gunshot kit or "GSW" kit.

Most officers, who have these kits, keep them in their vehicles, hopefully, within their reach. At my agency, we recommend a uniform location for the kit. Ideally, this is within reach of the officer sitting in the driver's seat. When it's uniformly stored, it also ensures anyone of us, during an emergency, can locate the kit no matter whose car we go to.

In Chapter Six, I will provide an example of a "GSW" kit successful use and a list of recommended items one should keep in the kit.

If the situation allows, and you have access to the filed dressing, follow these simple steps:

- Hold the field dressing above the exposed wound with the white side of the dressing material toward the wound.
- Pull on the tails so the dressing opens and flattens.
- Do not touch the white sterile side of the dressing.
- Place the dressing (white side) on the wound.
- Place one hand on top of the dressing to hold the dressing in place. Ask the officer to hold the dressing in place while you secure it.
- Tie the tails into a nonslip knot over the outer edge of the dressing, not over the wound itself.

- The bandage should be tight enough to keep the dressing from slipping, but not tight enough to interfere with blood circulation. You should be able to slip two fingers under the knot.

Check the circulation below the bandage. If the area below the bandage previously had adequate blood circulation but is now cool to the touch, bluish, or numb or if a pulse cannot be detected below the bandage, the bandage may be interfering with blood circulation. Loosen and retie the tails without disturbing the dressing. Recheck the circulation. If circulation is not restored, evacuate the casualty.

Applying a Pressure Dressing would be appropriate if blood continues to seep from the first dressing. A pressure dressing is applied only to a wound on an arm or leg.

When applying a Pressure Dressing over a Field Dressing, place a wad of material (folded shirt, cloth, etc.) on top of the dressing and directly over the wound. Apply the pressure dressing.

Tie the ends of the cravat in a nonslip knot directly over the wound. You should be able to insert the tip of one finger under the knot. Check the circulation below the pressure dressing. If the area below the pressure dressing previously had adequate blood circulation but is now cool to the touch, bluish, or numb or if a pulse can no longer be detected below the Pressure Dressing, loosen and retie the tails.

This method should not disturb any blood clot forming under the original dressing, which is the goal! Recheck the circulation. If circulation is not restored, evacuate the casualty. Apply manual pressure over the Pressure Dressing. If the wound continues to bleed, apply a tourniquet.

Application of a tourniquet

The tourniquet has always been a subject of controversy. As a matter fact, some agencies may not even allow the subject to be used or even trained. Until about three years ago, my agency experienced the same issue. When the concerns were identified to our staff, examples and supporting documentation was provided showing in our case specifically, the training and use of the tourniquet would be beneficial, the training and use was approved.

So, why are agencies reluctant to utilizing this tool? The most common concern I have heard is the liability.

This liability is simply translated into the concern that something may go wrong and a legal issue may be presented against the agency. When it comes to the tourniquet, and the category of "something may go wrong", the following concern has been expressed.

"The use of the tourniquet will cause the loss of limb"

Keep in mind that if you are in a situation where you need to apply a tourniquet to stop bleeding, your options are either bleed to death or risk the slim possibility of having a part of the body amputated.

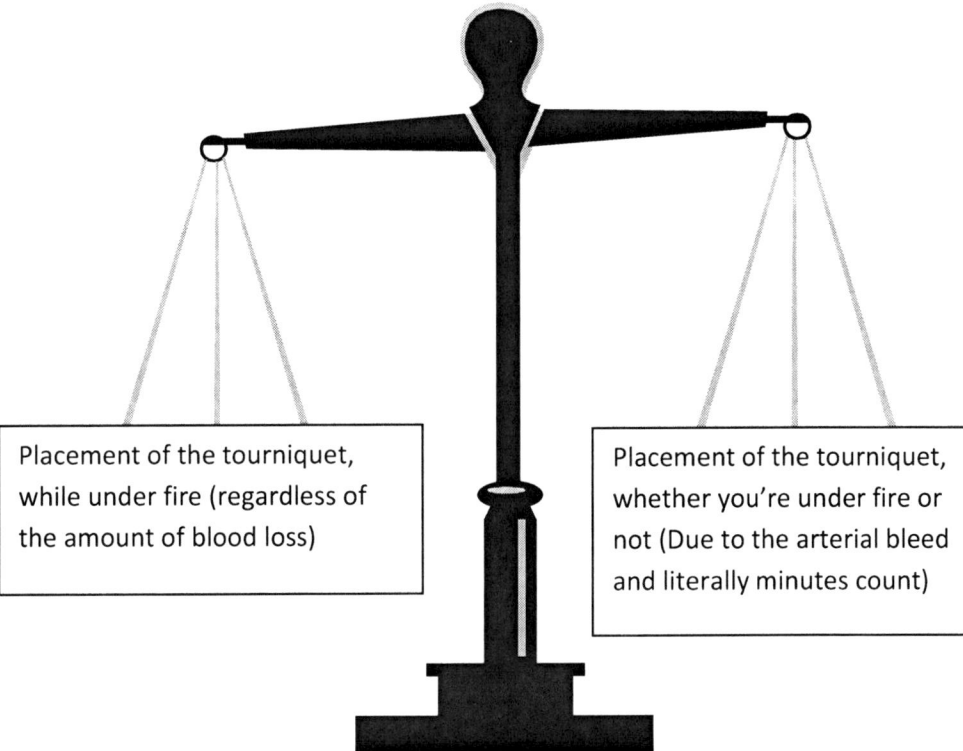

Placement of the tourniquet, while under fire (regardless of the amount of blood loss)

Placement of the tourniquet, whether you're under fire or not (Due to the arterial bleed and literally minutes count)

The key here is to be aware of the fact that in both of the examples given, the final results will be death if the tourniquet is not applied. On the left the officer quickly puts on a tourniquet, picks up his or her weapon and defends himself. On the right an officer applies a tourniquet because medical support is too far away.

In either case, the need to get to advance medical support as soon as possible is important.

To determine when a tourniquet is needed: (Again consider situation)

- Needed when a complete amputation of the upper arm, forearm, thigh, or lower leg has occurred (limb has been completely severed).
- Apply tourniquet to amputated limb without applying field and pressure dressings. Apply even if stump is not bleeding heavily.
- Do not apply for amputation of a part of a hand or part of a foot. Bleeding from these wounds can be controlled by a pressure dressing.
- Needed if the bleeding from a limb is severe and cannot be stopped by the application of a field dressing, manual pressure, elevation, and pressure dressing.
- If due to hostile fire, following the step by step recommendations to stop the bleeding, then go directly to the tourniquet and defend your life! Do not remove the tourniquet. Transport to advance life support and they will remove.

If you need an additional tourniquet or you don't have one yet, here is a guide that can help you quickly gather the materials to make a tourniquet band.

- Fold strong, pliable material (T-shirts, belts, seat belts, etc.) into a cravat at least two inches wide. **Do not use wire or shoestrings for a tourniquet band.**
- A rigid object- (I always recommend our batons) usually a stick, is used to tighten the tourniquet.
- Securing Materials (if needed) an additional cravat or securing material may be needed to secure the rigid object if the tourniquet band is not long enough.
- Padding- soft, smooth material to place between the limb and the tourniquet band. The casualty's shirt sleeve or trouser leg can be used.

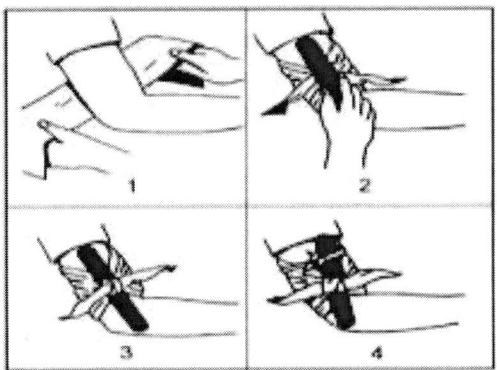

Select an upper arm or thigh site. If the wound is in the upper arm or thigh, select a site that is **two to four inches above** the edge of the wound or amputation site. This allows for the capture of the artery even after it contracts. If the wound is in the lower extremity, the ideal sites are still the upper arm and thigh just above the joint (elbow or knee).

Do not apply a tourniquet band over a joint or a fracture site. Imagine a water hose spraying water and violently moving. Think of your artery as that hose. When the tourniquet is applied correctly (tight enough) it compresses your tissue, muscle and artery against the bone. If dealing with a compound fracture, consider moving up higher.

Place padding around the limb where the tourniquet band will be applied to protect the skin from being pinched and twisted when the band is tightened. Smoothing the casualty's shirt sleeve or trouser leg over the tourniquet site is sufficient. Place the tourniquet band material around the tourniquet site. Tie the band with a half knot (like first part of tying a shoestring). Place the rigid object on top of the half knot. Tie a full knot that will not come undone over the rigid object.

Twist the rigid object (clockwise or counterclockwise) until the tourniquet is tight and the bright red bleeding has stopped. Generally, darker blood is from a vein and may continue to ooze even after the tourniquet has been properly applied. There should be no pulse below the tourniquet.

Wrap the tails of the tourniquet band around the end of the rigid object so the rigid object will not untwist, bring the tails under the limb, and tie the tails in a nonslip knot.

If the rigid object cannot be secured with the tails of the tourniquet band, wrap a piece of material around the limb below the tourniquet, wrap the material around one end of the rigid object so the tourniquet will not unwind, and tie the tails of the material in a nonslip knot.

Do not loosen the tourniquet once it is in place and has stopped the blood flow. Loosening the tourniquet band would allow the wound to start bleeding again, which could be fatal. Do not cover the tourniquet. Leave it in full view so it can be located quickly by medical personnel.

If the tourniquet is applied to an amputation, protect the amputation site (wound) from further contamination. Place a dressing made of soft, absorbent material over the end of the stump and secure the dressing with bandages.

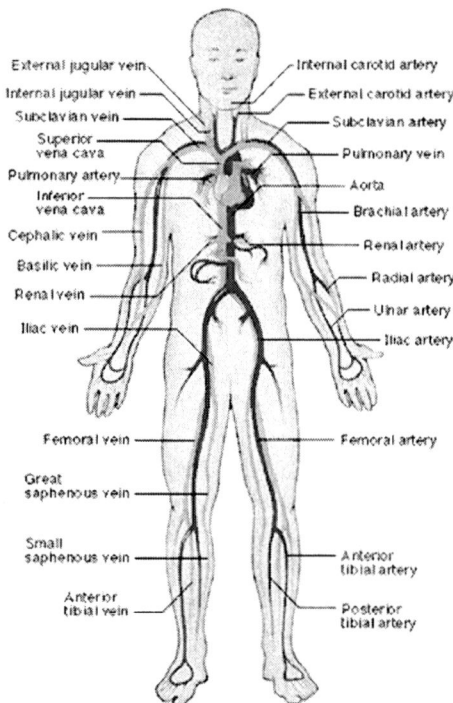

The arteries supply oxygenated blood throughout the body. The veins bring that de-oxygenated blood supply back through the lungs and heart. I recommend you **feel for, and locate your femoral and brachial arteries now**. Find them! Please don't wait for the day something happens, to assume you know how to do this.

Chapter 6

Recommendations for Assembling a "Gunshot Kit"

It is well known in the law enforcement community, money and time is always dedicated to the "cool toys" of the job. We get updated vehicles, weapons and technology but if one area has commonly failed to keep up, it is in our personal safety equipment. Sure, we keep all of the required safety equipment required by law (fire extinguishers, etc.), but what about personal protection for the officers?

"First-aid kits credited with saving lives in Tucson shooting"

TUCSON - Some of the first deputies to arrive at the scene of the Jan. 8 shooting rampage here described a scene of "silent chaos" on Friday, and they added that the carnage probably would have been much worse without the help of a $99 first-aid kit that recently became standard-issue.

Pima County Sheriff's Department deputies said they were dispatched to what they believed was a routine shooting. But when they arrived, they found a blood-drenched parking lot that looked more like the scene of a plane crash. Sgt. Gilberto Caudillo got on his radio and pleaded, "Send every ambulance you have out here."

"Innocent people looked like they were just massacred," Caudillo said Friday.

He was among about 10 sheriff's deputies who found themselves doing the duties of paramedics rather than police. In the six minutes before paramedics flooded the site, they had to staunch chest wounds, open injured airways, apply tourniquets and try to calm victims along with the blood-covered bystanders who tried to help. "We told them, 'All the bad stuff is over, you're safe. We'll stay by your side,' "said Deputy Matthew Salmon.

In the end, 13 of those shot survived, while six did not. One of the injured, Rep. Gabrielle Giffords (D-Ariz.) was the last person still hospitalized until Friday morning, when she was discharged and transported to a rehabilitation facility in Texas.

Doctors and law enforcement officials told reporters here that the incident would have been much worse without a small brown kit devised by David Kleinman, a SWAT team medic who had become concerned about rising violence.

Kleinman cobbled together the Individual First Aid Kits out of simple items used by combat medics in Iraq and Afghanistan. Included was an emergency bandage pioneered by the Israeli army; a strip of gauze that contains a substance which coagulates blood on contact; a tactical tourniquet, shears that are sturdy and sharp enough to slice off victims' clothing; and sealing material that works especially well on chest wounds.

The items in the kit were each inexpensive; the Israeli bandage, for example, cost only $6, but deputies reached for one "over and over at the scene," Kleinman said.

It is unusual for police officers to carry such medical equipment, but Capt. Byron Gwaltney, who coordinated the sheriff's office's response to the shooting, said it proved crucial in this case because the deputies were the first to arrive.

"It would have been a lot worse" without those tools, Gwaltney said. The deputies were trained to use the kit, in a program the Pima force called "First Five Minutes," six months ago.

The deputies who initially responded said they were not the ones who arrested the suspect, Jared Lee Loughner. Instead, their focus was conducting triage through the parking lot: figuring out who was dead, who was injured and who was simply a helpful person who had jumped in to help.

They used the tourniquets and gauze to stop the bleeding. They used a chest seal, also in the kit, to close bullet wounds. They used the shears in the kit to cut off the victims' clothes.

"When I look back, I don't know if we drowned out the moans to focus or if it was quiet," said Deputy Ryan Inglett, who treated several victims with combat gauze and assisted in CPR. "This is something I will never forget."

By Sandhya Somashekhar and Sari Horwitz
Washington Post Staff Writers
Friday, January 21, 2011; 9:57 PM

The first gunshot kit I remember receiving at my agency was in a black zippered pouch, sealed with a zip-tie. Of course, I was very grateful for receiving one, but I was concerned.

I really had no idea what was in the kit and the zip-tie only suggested that I should not open it. When I asked questions about the contents, I was told that I have all that I really needed in case I was shot.

Of course, sometime later, I open the bag only to find an extremely large gauze and a few other simple items. Thankfully, that has all changed and we now provide our deputies with more appropriate equipment.

If you do a little research on the internet, you will find many companies who have gunshot kits for sale. The following is a list of recommended items which can be purchased individually and easily made in to a kit.

- Compression bandage (aka Israeli bandage or Cedderoth Blood-Stopper)
- Compressed gauze
- Asherman Chest Seal (for penetrating trauma to the chest)
- Hemostatic gauze (Quik-Clot)
- Nasopharyngeal airway and lube
- C.A.T. Tourniquet (recommended to be carried on your person)
- EMT shears

And yes, the kits are as I mentioned before copied out of military doctrine and training driven by recent experiences in Iraq and Afghanistan.

No matter what your choices are, you must allow yourself to train with them. "Let us not lose any officers, because he or she could not open a package, understand instructions or put on a tourniquet!"

The name "blow-out" kit is a bit of dark humor, as they are used to "patch & plug leaks" in humans caused by penetrating trauma, much as rubber patches and glue were used to patch & plug leaks in blown-out tires.

Chapter 7

Techniques for Moving Casualties

<u>Moving Casualties</u>

The primary purpose of all rescue work is to get injured people out of danger and to medical help as quickly as possible. If you have never attempted to physically move another person, you will be surprised to learn that it is not always as easy as it looks.

Like with anything else, being aware of a technique may not always be enough. If you're not already familiar with the techniques described here, pair up with another person and try them. It is important to know what your abilities are in order to avoid injury to yourself and the person your training with.

It has always been my recommendation to learn as many carries as you can, but choose one or two that you (due to body type, strength, etc.) can perform. Sure, it would be great if we could all just grab any person regardless of height, weight and location and just throw them over our shoulder and go. Realistically, we know that is not going to happen. What we do know is that with a little practice and perhaps some minor modifications to a particular technique, we can perform the rescue and even provide lethal cover if needed.

As discussed before, your rescue plan has to be quick, incorporating many decisions. Part of that decision making may include how to get an officer out of danger. For example, Jan 2011, the St. Petersburg Police Department, City of St. Petersburg, Florida had officers wounded both inside and outside of a residence, the suspect intentionally utilizes a mortally wounded officer (unconfirmed at the time) as bait. In a case like this, one person cannot safely perform this type of rescue.

When we, as law enforcement, categorize the types of rescues that can be performed by a police officer, often "Self-Rescue" is over looked. We should nurture the warrior mindset from the beginning (during training). If you noticed, I stated, "rescues that can be performed by a police officer". This is important. If you were to survey the many types of drags and carries that have been created and employed, you will see that a vast majority of them, while still applicable, require equipment, lots of practice and more than one person.

So, reasonably speaking, it would be beneficial to identify those carries which can be done with the equipment you're going to have with you.

If you're a patrol officer, then you're limited to what you may have on hand as opposed to a tactical medic or a fire fighter.

If you're the officer confronted with this threat, self-rescue is included in the immediate reaction as discussed before.

- Return fire and take cover immediately (no specific order).
- Remain engaged by defending or taking action against the suspect if appropriate (avoid additional wounds).
- Control hemorrhages through self-aid if able.
- If threat is still present and engaging, one handed direct pressure or a quick application of a tourniquet can be used to control the blood loss.
- Continually assess, move if needed and communicate to dispatch.

<u>One-rescuer methods</u>

Single person rescue or "one-rescuer" methods are what most officers assigned to a patrol function want to know. Whether it is a citizen or a fellow officer, it does not matter. Patrol officers are often alone and have to react immediately to what they have. Below are some simple concepts and techniques.

Never move the casualty any further than needed. Scan the escape route(s) to determine the best method and route to carry or drag the casualty. Because you're alone, you must move the casualty quickly.

Examples of rescues techniques (obviously just a few).

<u>Drag</u>

This method, at the very least, is the immediate response to an ambush style attack, where you have just realized that your partner is not responding and still in the line of fire. It is the slowest and requires lots of brute strength compared to other techniques. This method is usually conducted one handed allowing you to have your weapon drawn and assuming all of the tactical responsibility.

The drag factor, weight, obstacles, distance to cover as well as your strength are all considerations. With the drag technique, your focus is not so much the technique itself, but the immediate removal of the officer out of the line of fire. I often tell our students, you have to grab what you can grab, even if it just a foot, and just go!

Drag carry

This carry is used to drag a casualty after you have repositioned him/her to either lying on their back or in a sitting position. Quickly position your hands under the casualty's shoulders (arms) and grasp the clothing on each side, supporting the head between your forearms.

Prior to conducting your lift, be aware of your back and lift with your legs. Drag the casualty backward only as far as necessary for his/her safety. Be careful, ensuring not to choke the casualty while pulling on their clothing. Keep in mind, this technique will not allow you to provide lethal cover. If your casualty is conscious order him or her to draw their weapon and provide cover while you're moving.

Blanket drag

An alternate method to the drag carries, where the rescuer can use a blanket to support some of the weight and pull the casualty. With this method, you are using whatever you can find immediately around you and your casualty. The technique is referred to as the blanket drag, but you don't have to limit yourself to a blanket. An abandoned tarp, a rain coat or anything of suitable size will do here.

This is good problem solving technique for body size factors which present physical challenges. Again if it can be accomplished one handed, this is best which allows you to draw your weapon and provide cover.

Pick-a-back

If your casualty is conscious, simply lift the casualty from a standing or sitting position onto your back. Lean forward and support their weight with your lower back. If the casualty is unconscious and you can lift the person, position the casualty on their back, lift their knees up and move their feet close to their buttocks, cross grab with both hands, lift and turn.

The goal is to end up in the Pick-a back position. Keep in mind if arm injuries are extensive, this technique may be difficult to accomplish.

Removal Downstairs

If this removal must be conducted immediately, then your main concern of course, is to get out line of fire. At the very least and if at all possible, you should consider protecting the casualty's head during this rescue.

This decision of course, will be determined by the circumstance you find yourself in. If you are not in the line of fire and are trying to move the casualty to medical care, then one of the previous carries would be more practical.

If the casualty is too heavy to lift alone, consider the use of a rug or a mattress if one is available.

Human crutch

This method is only for casualties who can help themselves. It is an easy and fast way to move the less seriously injured out of harm's way. With this method, you are the crutch, supporting the injured person's injured side and sharing the tactical responsibly. Don't assume your victim cannot walk. Ask them if they can. You may save yourself a lot of effort.

Two-rescuer methods

If there are two rescuers to do the carrying, try one of these emergency methods:

(Remember, modifications to these techniques can be made while considering your physical abilities and need to provide lethal cover).

Chair lift

The chair carry can be used for a conscious or unconscious casualty but not for suspected head/spinal injuries if not under fire. For protection, secure the casualty's hands across his or her chest and, if the casualty is unconscious, secure the person to the chair.

Two-hand seat carry

The two-hand seat carry is another way to carry a conscious casualty who can neither walk nor support their upper body. Make a hook with your fingers by folding them towards your palm and grab onto your partner's "hook". This makes a seat for the casualty to sit on while using your other arm to support their shoulders in an upright position.

Multi-rescuer methods

If there are more than two of you to do the job, there are a number of methods which can be used to carry casualties. This also allows plenty of options to address any potential threats.

Blanket lift

- Roll a blanket or rug lengthwise for half its width. Position rescuers at the head and feet to keep the head, neck and body in line.
- Kneel at the casualty's shoulder and position a bearer at the waist to help logroll the casualty onto the uninjured side. Turn the casualty as a unit so that his/her body is not twisted during the log roll.
- Roll the casualty back over the blanket roll to lay face up on the blanket.
- Unroll the blanket and then roll the edges of the blanket to each side of the casualty, creating a grip point. Prepare to lift the casualty – have officers grip the rolls at the head and shoulders, the hips and legs.
- Keep the blanket tight as the casualty is lifted and move to cover.

Three-person lift and carry

This is an excellent way of lifting a badly hurt person without complicating most injuries. Using this, the casualty can be carried forward, sideways or lowered onto a stretcher.

Improvised stretchers

If a commercially prepared stretcher is not available, you can improvise one by using a tabletop, door, two rigid poles and a blanket or clothing. Don't use non-rigid stretchers for casualties with suspected head or spinal injuries.

Blanket and poles stretcher

- Place the blanket flat on the ground and place a pole one-third of the way from the end. Fold the one-third length of the blanket over the pole.
- Place the second pole parallel to the first so that it is on the doubled part of the blanket, about 15 cm (6 in) from the doubled edge.
- Fold the remaining blanket over the two poles. The casualty's weight on the blanket holds the folds in place.

Stretchers from found materials

Doors, short ladders, sheets of galvanized metal, etc. can all be used to improvise stretchers. Keep an eye out for suitable materials.

Make sure the stretcher and casualty will clear passageways and that the stretcher is strong enough to hold the casualty.

NOTE: Test an improvised stretcher with someone of equal or heavier weight than the casualty to ensure that it will hold. Check the clearance of an improvised stretcher to ensure it will pass through hallways, doors and stairways without harm to the casualty.

Lashing casualty to stretcher

Whenever casualties have to be carried over uneven ground or debris, they should be lashed to the stretcher using the straps provided by the equipment. If you are working with found materials, use what you can to secure your casualty.

Carrying stretchers

A stretcher should be carried by at least four people; normally facing the direction of travel, with the casualty's feet first. When traveling uphill, upstairs or loading into a vehicle they should carry head first. Remind rescuers to watch the casualty while they are transporting them for any changes in condition.

Uneven ground and obstacles

When crossing uneven ground, a stretcher should be carried by four people and kept as level as possible. The rescuers must adjust the height of the stretcher to compensate for dips and rises in the terrain.

If the ground is unstable, the stretcher should be passed along a row of six to eight people rather than have bearers move over the rubble – especially when set down – since the lashing could tighten around the casualty.

If going through a doorway, the front bearers should move to the middle of the stretcher and let the front part protrude through the door. One rescuer at a time moves through the doorway, and then re-grasps the stretcher.

Avoid crossing over walls or high obstacles, even if it means a longer carry. Where a wall must be crossed, follow these steps:

- Lift the stretcher so the front handles are supported by the wall. The people in the rear hold the stretcher level while the front person crosses the wall.
- All officers lift together and move the stretcher forward until the rear handles rest on the wall. The people in the rear then cross the wall.

Any casualty who has been injured may experience increased distress and pain as a result of rescue efforts. Remember, never move the casualty any further than necessary to find cover and wait for additional help. Do only what is necessary to ensure the casualty's safety and to preserve life. Continue to reassure the conscious casualty and when possible, have someone stay with him/her until help arrives.

In any rescue or multiple casualty situations, confusion and chaos will likely be present. It is essential that individuals charged with helping injured people be able to remain calm and act quickly but carefully. Rescuers must always be observant for potential hazards to either themselves or other people in the area.

In a situation where you suspect a possible head or spinal injury has occurred, if the life of the casualty is not under immediate threat, seek the help of specialists before attempting to move the injured. If movement is essential but your life is not in danger, attempt to maintain normal anatomical alignment for the casualty (nose, belly button, inside of ankles). If the person is not in this position, get the help of qualified medical personnel.

In a mass-casualty event, try to establish quickly how many casualties are involved. Go to the nearest casualty, provided it is safe, and check for responsiveness. If the person does not answer you or respond to your attempts to wake them, check to see if the person is breathing. Your aim is to keep the casualty alive until medical help arrives. Do not waste time dealing with minor injuries until all casualties have been found and stabilized.

If the person is not breathing, and you're not in the line of fire, begin artificial respiration until help gets arrives. If the casualty is bleeding severely, apply either a pressure bandage/tourniquet, whichever is applicable. Remember, time is valuable. Give first aid for life-threatening conditions quickly perform the rescue!

Chapter 8

Scenario Based, Realistic and Dynamic Training

Training! How many books, articles, opinions and concepts have your heard out there? It seems everyone has their own philosophy on what training should be and how it should be conducted.

No matter how you look at it, tactical casualty care under fire, addresses a moment in time which requires your immediate reaction and responses to a deadly attack. To assume that being exposed to a four-hour block of instruction in a classroom setting is enough, would be a huge misunderstanding of how your mind and body reacts to these types of emergencies.

The concept of muscle memory addresses this and shows how anyone with sufficient practice can perform a certain task, a certain way under stress. An example of this would be, when you are given new holster, you're told to make your weapon safe and draw out of the holster repeatedly to break the holster in.

However, unlike what is required to break your holster in, preparing for an ambush style attack, or a rescue of another, requires much more involvement.

If you think about it, your muscle memory response is not the only factor. How about the emotional and logical aspects? Can you overcome the emotional barriers of witnessing your own injuries or the injuries of another officer? Would you logically allow yourself to get drawn into a potentially deadly situation, often referred to as "Tombstone courage"? These are in fact very difficult questions to answer for anyone, unless you have experienced it.

Realistically, there are only two ways that you're going to "experience" such an event. One is by actually being at the live call and the second, through training.

So, how much training is required to become "proficient" at the skills needed to enhance your survival rate during care under fire? As much and as many times as you can!

It was the great eighteenth century Russian field marshal Aleksandr Vasilevich Suvorov (1729-1800), who first said, "Train hard, fight easy." This is a quote that is commonly stated in tactical training settings. As trainers, our ultimate mission is to keep the officers we train alive.

Receiving emails and letters from survivors of violent encounters is the proof and the ultimate payback for our dynamic and realistic training.

Training should teach officers not just how to handle weapons, but how to handle situations. That's the bottom line: realistic, dynamic training gives officers the tools they need in order to survive and prevail in the real world. Realistic, dynamic training encourages officers think for themselves, realize mistakes and to push themselves further and harder than they have ever done before.

It identifies areas of concern that would have not been identified in a classroom environment. The shocked expressions seen on your officer's face when a scenario surprises them with an equipment limitation or failure issue, a physical inability or lack of understanding is a sign of learning.

It incorporates lessons learned from past and recent related events. Let's take firearms training as an example. Most police officers qualify once a year. They do so by shooting on a range in daylight and maybe some low light, but at a target from a fixed position. In the real world and lust looking at the FBI's 2010 report, most officer-related shootings take place in low light, with both the officer and the perpetrator frantically trying to find cover and protect themselves. In most officer-related shootings, the proper use of cover and concealment is critical to officer survival. But cover, concealment, low light, and shooting on the move are rarely incorporated in their training as opposed to meeting the standard of the qualification process.

It should incorporate a building block approach (separate each individual task, repeat until proficient, before exposing to multiple tasks in a scenario). The building block approach insures that your officers understand the concepts and goals, the use and application and when it should be applied, this is extremely important.

Lessons plans are very helpful in the planning stages of the course. It allows you to have an overview of the building block approach; it should cover everything from your introduction in the classroom to your final scenarios in the field. Some of the items that are commonly used in a lesson plan are:

- Course title and length
- Primary and alternate instructors
- Learning goals and training objectives
- Time lines and scenario scripts
- Equipment, training locations and safety.

Realistic and dynamic training

Here is where it all comes together. With a solid foundation of the concepts, goals and application, a good understanding of previous events and the ability to think out of the box and look for other potential outcomes, realistic and dynamic training can be achieved. During this type of training many aspects of police training come together. From report writing, to firearms training, to defensive tactics etc. Will you have the answer to all of the possibilities that may exist? Of course not. But with as many examples and variables that you can provide, you will at the very least give your officers plenty to refer back to.

An example of this would be to create a scenario where the officer gets injured while sitting in his or her patrol vehicle (after all it's where we spend a lot of time). Rather than just beginning the scenario with this idea, incorporate it into something realistic like a traffic stop, arriving at a call, or just parked and typing a report. Incorporate legal requirements and departmental SOP's. Be cautious to stay within the learning goals and training objectives and not go off onto another topic that can be time consuming.

Allow for as many officer responses as you can. Many times a good training program is one that has been presented many times over. This allows for all of the potential outcomes (that were not previously identified) to surface and be addressed. More importantly, any safety concerns that may have not been considered can be addressed.

Insure that a good amount of stress is incorporated into the training. Stress can be a variation of a time constraint to a problem solving issue. It can involve more than one suspect, or one that can't be seen. It can be physical as much as psychological (fully uniformed officer as a casualty).

Dress rehearsal? There are some advantages to training with and without your issued equipment. You should be very comfortable with the way your equipment is going to affect your movement and abilities. It makes no sense to spend hours upon hours in a classroom getting CPR training without field scenarios. You may find that during a building search (for example) your officer is so ramped up that he or she will never remember how to perform CPR correctly when they find a downed officer or even forget that the downed officer is wearing a ballistic vest prior to performing chest compressions.

Too much equipment? We all have seen them! The officer who has to have it all!

In order for the realistic portion of this concept to be effective, guidance should be given to those officers that carry way too much. Help them identify equipment that will be essential to their survival. Sometimes the only way to do this is to help them realize these themselves thru scenario training.

The same would have to be said for the officer that does not carry enough or their issued equipment. The concern here wouldn't be whether or not he or she has enough room on their gun belt because of their small frame, rather complacency instead.

Complacent thinking, perceived convenience and the pursuit for "comfort" have become reasons why I see this occurring. It takes a dedicated training team to agree on identifying these concerns and addressing them appropriately. Whether it's done indirectly through scenario based training or directly by way of suggestions or counseling, it should be addressed.

An example of this would be an officer removing a less lethal weapon for a cell phone, or simply has made a voluntary willful decision not to carry any less lethal weapons at all. An indirect way to address this would be to have one of your scenarios incorporate a transition from lethal to less lethal or less lethal to lethal. Introduce several decision making drills that will involve less lethal options.

This is not done in a malicious fashion, nor is the officer singled out. However, each officer is provided quick feedback, ending in positive form and allowing them to realize and state the disadvantages.

There is a fine balance between realistic scenario based training and training perceived as unlikely to happen or unwinnable. Utilizing events that have recently occurred throughout the world creates validity for your training. Open ended questions or suggestions that allow officers to think about what could also happen can be useful as well.

Quality control! The ability to provide all of your officers with the same training is important. For officers it's important to know that everyone is getting the same information. An easy way to accomplish this would be to set up training stations. Assign enough instructor(s) to each scenario with the scripted outline. Keep it simple, but keep it consistent. Eventually, the scripts will be memorized.

This is by no means saying that you cannot be flexible. Allow acceptable outcomes for your scenarios. Set up options for the officers. Don't make them obvious, but do go over them briefly during a class feedback.

For example: you have a female that is given a scenario where she has to immediately drag a heavy male out of the line fire. It's apparent that she may not physically be able to use brute strength, but with the help of a blanket for example, she can reduce the drag factor and therefore reduce the amount of strength needed. This blanket could just be place at the training site as a prop.

If your scenario has an option like this in place, and most of your students missed it, then don't discuss this during your short brief backs. Address the subject at the end so that all of the students can benefit from the learning opportunity. Focus on your training goals and objectives.

Feedback. This is obviously important. Officers will be looking for acknowledgement during all of their phases of the training. Allow for a really quick feedback to each of the officers performance during the scenario. You could do something as simple as pointing out a negative action or two, but definitely wrap it up by ending a positive action or two.

Do not dwell on non-training issues (remember goals and objectives). If need to, make note and arrange a separate time for the same. Here you want to provide officers with the sense that they have or well on the way to grasping the concepts and applying them appropriately.

As in any training event, careful thought to agency policy violations, legal requirements and civil violations should be discussed and reviewed prior by the training staff and during the presentation by the officers. An example would be your agencies deadly force policy. It should be well understood by all of the certified staff.

CHAPTER 9

Example Lesson Plan

COURSE: Introduction to Tactical Casualty Care (Under fire) for Law Enforcement.

HOURS: 4.0

FILE NUMBER: 0001

PREPARED BY: Deputy/Officer Anyone

DATE PREPARED: 01/30/2010

PRIMARY INST: Deputy/Officer Anyone

ALTERNATE INST: Deputy/Officer Others

LEARNING GOAL: To provide law enforcement personal with the concepts of tactical casualty care, create an understanding on how it directly relates to Police Officers. Provide Life-saving skills and how and when it should be applied.

SUMMARY OF TRAINING OBJECTIVES:
1. Introduce the goals and concepts of Tactical Casualty Care and how it relates to the Law Enforcement community.
2. Identify the three stages of care during a critical incident and factors that influence this care.
3. Distinguish the difference between a life threatening and a non-life threatening injury. Understanding how, when and where to treat a life threatening and a non-life threatening injury.
4. Introduce the application and use of a Tourniquet, Israeli Bandage and Occlusive bandage.
5. Provide recommendations for assembling a "Gunshot Kit".
6. Become familiar with techniques required for moving an injured Officer/Deputy to safety.

Training Objectives:
Upon completion of this course, the Officer/Deputy will have the knowledge required to provide treatment of life and non-life threatening injuries, to themselves or to another person.

1. Students will have an understanding of what "Tactical Casualty Care (Under Fire)" is and how the "Warrior mindset" plays an important role.
2. Students will become better prepared to identify what types of injuries are life threatening and non-threatening.
3. Students will quickly assess and treat any life-threatening injuries at the appropriate time to avoid further casualties.
4. Students will be familiar with a "trauma pack" as well as the recommended contents (Quick Clot, Israeli Field Dressing, 4X4 bandage, Vaseline gauze).
5. Students will be familiar with "Tactical Field Care" and "Casualty Evacuation" concepts.

Course Introduction:
To be presented with the assigned power point presentation.
Video: 2nd slide
(Quote): Article "The Relevance of Tactical Combat Casualty Care (TCCC) Guidelines to Civilian Law Enforcement Operations
By Kevin B. Gerold, DO, JD; Capt. Mark Gibbons, EMT-P; and Sean McKay, EMT-P

Opening Statement: (NOTE: use an example the class will relate to)
On October 9th 2001 2210hrs, Cpl. Terry Metts is dispatched to a shots fired call in the Lealman area of Pinellas County. During the initial stages of this call, Cpl. Metts is shot with a high powered rifle. Cpl. Metts advises that he is shot in his arm and bleeding profusely. The efforts to rescue Cpl. Metts were initially hampered due to the fact that the responding deputies were pinned down by gun fire. Cpl. Metts was able to apply direct pressure to his wounds and despite severe blood loss, was able to survive this incident. Cpl. Metts also recognized the onset of shock and was able to combat this and maintain his composure in a tense situation.

* It is incidents like this one that demonstrate a need to train in and practice tactical casualty care under fire techniques for themselves or other members.

Three basic goals to the concept of Casualty Care Under Fire:
- Save preventable deaths
- Prevent additional casualties
- Complete the mission (Rescue)

This approach recognizes a particularly important principle:

- Performing the correct intervention at the correct time while under fire.
- A medically correct intervention at the wrong time in a situation may lead to further casualties.

Stages of care:

- Care Under Fire (This intro course will focus on the stage).
- Tactical Field Care
- Casualty Evacuation Care

Student will have an understanding of what Tactical Casualty Care (under Fire) is and how the "warrior mindset" plays an important role.

- Tactical Casualty Care is the care rendered by the officer to him/herself or by another officer performing a rescue at the point of where the injury(s) occurred while under effective hostile fire.
- The "Warrior Mindset" the thinking that one will not ever give up or ever die, is important during this event. It may be the difference between death (giving up) and survival (never giving up).

Tactical Field Care:

- Tactical Field Care" is the care rendered by the medic once no longer under effective hostile fire.
- Also applies to situations in which an injury has occurred, but there has been no hostile fire.
- Available medical equipment still limited to that carried into the field by medical personnel or TEMS.
- Time to evacuation may vary considerably.

Member will have a better understanding on how to identifying a life threatening injury or non-life threatening injury.

- Sick or Not Sick

- The average adult male has 4 to 5 quarts of blood in the body. Typically blood pressure begins to drop (hypotension) when 20 – 30% is lost. Death can occur when 40% of blood loss occurs and the volume is not replaced.

- There are five areas where people can bleed large amounts causing shock. They are the chest, abdomen, pelvis, long bones (e.g. Femur) and extremities.

- Capillary Bleeding- When a minor scrape or cut opens some capillaries; the bleeding is almost always very slow and small in quantity. Your body's natural clotting mechanism is able to stop most cases of capillary bleeding within seconds to minutes.

-
- Venous Bleeding- Deep cuts have the potential to cut open veins. A cut vein typically results in a steady but relatively slow flow of dark red blood. The best way to stop most cases of venous bleeding is to put direct pressure on the wound.

- Arterial Bleeding- This is the least common and most dangerous type of bleeding. It involves bright red blood that comes out in large volume, and in spurts that correspond with each beat of your heart.

Member will understand how to evaluate, when and to treat a life threatening or non-life threatening injury.
- 3 Risk Phases (Approach, Aid and Extraction)
- Field dressings, pressure dressing and tourniquets

Deputies will be familiar with a recommended first aid kit, (Gunshot), which is currently used by many agencies throughout the country.
- Compression bandage (Israeli bandage or Cedderoth Blood-Stopper)
- Compressed gauze
- Asherman Chest Seal (for penetrating trauma to the chest)
- Hemostatic gauze (Quik-Clot)
- Nasopharyngeal airway and lube
- C.A.T. Tourniquet (recommended to be carried on your person)
- EMT shears

Definitions:

1.   **Tactical Field Care** - the care rendered by the deputy once he and the casualty is no longer under effective hostile fire. If also applies to situations in which an injury has occurred, but there has been no hostile fire. Available medical equipment is still limited to that carried into the field by the deputies or medical personnel assigned to the team.

2. **Care Under Fire** - the care rendered by a deputy at the scene of the injury while he and the casualty are still under effective hostile fire. Available medical equipment is limited to that carried by the soldier or the medic on their person, or in the medic's aid bag.

3. **First Aid** - The immediate Aid given to a casualty prior to the arrival of medical personnel. (EMS)

4. **Non-life threatening injuries** - Injuries that will not require an immediate action by the injured or another to sustain life. (NOT SICK)

5. **Life threatening injuries** - injuries which will require an immediate action by an injured person or another, in order to prevent death. (SICK)

References:

- Trauma and Gunshot wounds: What you need to know to save a life. Dr. Maurizio A. Miglietta.
- Law and Order Magazine vol.57 page 27 "Training for Gunshot Wound Treatment".

CHAPTER 10

Example Scenario Script With Time Line

Introduction to Tactical Casualty Care under fire (For Law Enforcement)

Course Length: 4.0 Hours
Minimum Staff: 2
Equipment: CAT Tourniquet, Israeli Bandage, (1 per every two students) and 1 CPR training mannequin.
Location: Anywhere training center, classroom # and mock apartment.
Course Outline:
- 1600 hours: Student reception, Staff Introductions and course description and intent.
- 1700 hours: Student break, student organization in pairs for practical application exercises.
- 1800 hours: Step by Step instruction and concepts for immediate application for equipment, student break.
- 1900 hours: Scenario based training. 3-4 scenarios based on class size. Students break while not actively involved in scenarios.
- 1945-2000 hours: Course feedback and conclusion.

Summary: 1st two hours, classroom with concepts and practical exercises. 2nd two hours, step by step application and scenarios.

Scenario 1: (1student, GSW at a door, **venous bleed**, and threat still exists.)

>Student will arrive at home for a 911 hang up call with little or no information. Nothing is herd by the student upon the approach to the home's door.
>
>Upon arrival at the door, student is told that a gunshot is herd, and realizes that he/she has been knocked back to the ground away from the door. Student is also told that he/she has gunshot wound which produced a venous bleed to the left forearm and can now hear a subject behind the close door, unlocking the deadbolts.

Student should:

1. Make a rapid retreat to cover and concealment, while alerting dispatch. Address the threat if the subject comes out of the home (one handed).
2. Make a quick assessment of the injury(s).
3. Choose the most appropriate lifesaving technique for the injury(s).
4. Defend until additional units arrive, establish communication, establish your location and perform a rescue if needed.

Scenario 2: (2 students, GSW outside of home, **Arterial bleed** and threat still exists.)

1st Student will be arriving at home for a 911 hang up call with little or no information. No updates are provided or available by the dispatcher upon arrival to the call. What is considered a tactically sound decision is made by parking several homes away and across the street.

The 1st student is told that upon approach to the home, a gunshot is herd, and falls back on to the ground. 1st student is told that a severe injury to the left leg with an arterial bleed has occurred and has notified dispatch to warn any incoming units. 1st student still stunned is trying to drag themselves back towards a vehicle for cover. 2nd student arrives, tells 1st student to stop moving, and places vehicle between line of fire and 1st student. 2nd student is asked to apply the most appropriate lifesaving technique while the potential of further threat is addressed.

Student(s) should:

1. 1st student should explain why the need to retreat to cover and concealment, while alerting dispatch.
2. 2nd student should develop a plan to rescue 1st student.
3. Make a quick assessment of the injury(s).
4. Choose the most appropriate lifesaving technique for the injury(s).
5. Both students should discuss options to defend while care is provided and rescue plan.

Scenario 3: (1student, GSW, **arterial bleed**, and threat no longer exist.)

Same as scenario #1, threat was stopped, arterial bleed to arm.

Scenario 4: (2 students, GSW outside of home, **Arterial bleed** and not breathing threat still exists.)

Same as scenario #2, CPR required after rescue.

--------------------End of Scripts/ 4hr lesson plan--------------------

Here is an example of a performance check list that can be used.

Combat Application Tourniquet (C-A-T)

Objective: Demonstrate the proper application of a Combat Application Tourniquet.

Evaluation: Students will be evaluated as a Pass/Fail (P/F). The instructor will verify the student's ability to quickly and effectively apply a Combat Application Tourniquet to an extremity of him/herself or a fellow student by observing the student's procedure and technique.

Materials: Student Checklists, Combat Application Tourniquets (one per student)

Provide each instructor with Student Checklists.

Instructor Guidelines:
- Ensure each student has all required materials.
- Read the Learning Objective and the evaluation method to the student.
- Explain the grading of the exercise.

Performance Steps:

1. Remove the C-A-T from the carrying pouch.
2. Slide the extremity through the loop of the Self-Adhering Band or wrap Self-Adhering Band around the extremity and reattach to friction adapter buckle.
3. Position the C-A-T above the wound; leave at least 2 inches of uninjured skin between the C-A-T and the wound.
4. Secure the C-A-T.
5. Pull the free running end of the Self-Adhering Band tight and securely fasten it back on itself (if applying to an arm wound). Do not adhere the band past the Windlass Clip. - If applying to a leg wound, the Self-Adhering Band must be routed through both sides of the friction adapter buckle and fastened back on itself. This will prevent it from loosening when twisting the Windlass Clip.
6. Twist the Windlass Rod until the bleeding stops. When the tactical situation permits insure the distal pulse is no longer palpable.
7. Lock the rod in place with the Windlass Clip.

INSTRUCTOR: Monitor the distal pulse, and prompt the student when it is no longer palpable.

NOTE: Use care to not let the student over-tighten the C-A-T. If pain becomes too severe, discontinue the tourniquet application.

- Grasp the Windlass Strap, pull it tight and adhere it to the Velcro on the Windlass Clip. : For added security (and always before moving the casualty), secure the Windlass Rod with the Windlass Strap. For smaller extremities, continue to wind the Self-Adhering Band across the Windlass Clip and secure it under the Windlass Strap.

NOTE: On a real casualty, the date and time the C-A-T was applied would be recorded when tactically feasible (applies for cases where officers work in remote areas).

NOTE: A real casualty's wound would be dressed, and the casualty would be transported to definitive treatment as dictated by the tactical situation.

Remove the C-A-T from the carrying pouch.

P / F

Slide the wounded extremity through the loop of the Self-Adhering Band or wrap around extremity.

    P / F

Positioned the C-A-T above simulated wound site; left at least 2 inches of uninjured skin between the C-A-T and the wound site.

    P / F

Twist the Windlass Rod until the distal pulse was no longer palpable.

    P / F

Lock the rod in place with the Windlass Clip.

    P / F

Grasped the Windlass Strap, pulled it tight and adhered it to the Velcro on the Windlass Clip.

    P / F

Verbalized using a marker to draw a "T" on the casualty's forehead and recorded the date and time the C-A-T was applied.

    P / F

Objective: Demonstrate how to drag/carry a casualty.

Evaluation: Students will be evaluated as a Pass/Fail (P/F). The instructor will verify the accuracy of the student's ability to drag/carry a casualty by means of observing the student's procedures and technique.

Materials: Student or mannequin in their dress uniform if feasible

Student Checklists

- Provide each instructor with Student Checklists.

Instructor Guidelines:

- Ensure each student has all required materials.
- Read the Learning Objective and the evaluation method to the student.
- Explain the grading of the exercise.

Performance Steps:

- Determine appropriate carry for tactical situation, estimated distance, and number of rescuers. This drag is for short distances.

One-person drag P/F
- Secure weapon as feasible.
- Grasp casualty by equipment with 1 or 2 hands.
- Begin drag.

Determine appropriate carry for tactical situation, estimated distance, and number of rescuers. Drag can be high or low profile

Two-person drag P/F

- Communicate plan with team member before attempting drag.
- Secure weapon and other equipment as feasible.
- Each member secures casualty by equipment with one hand.
- Begin drag.

ABOUT THE AUTHOR

Current Status

Deputy Rafael Navarro is currently serving in the Law enforcement Training Division of the Pinellas County Sheriff's Office, Florida.

History and specialty

Deputy Rafael Navarro is a retired SFC/E7, United States Army; Military Police Corps. He has been in law enforcement since 2000; he has served 4 years with his agencies SWAT team, 3 years in the Community Policing Unit.

Credentials

Deputy Rafael Navarro is a certified evaluator/instructor for Defensive Tactics, ASP, Firearms, Vehicle operations, Advanced Taser & Taser X26, Chemical munitions, less-lethal, flash bang and Aerosol certification. Basic submachine gun certification and Basic SWAT school certification.

Special Note

Deputy Rafael Navarro Retired SFC/E-7 after 21 years of military service with the United States Army, Military Police Corps, and 24 months in Afghanistan in support of combat operations during Operation Enduring Freedom; Recipient of a Bronze Star.

CPSIA information can be obtained at www.ICGtesting.com
Printed in the USA
LVOW130513120712

289707LV00005B/30/P